Jellyfish

BY KARA L. LAUGHLIN

The Child's World®
childsworld.com

Published by The Child's World®
1980 Lookout Drive • Mankato, MN 56003-1705
800-599-READ • www.childsworld.com

DESIGN ELEMENTS
© creatOR76/Shutterstock.com: porthole
© keren-seg/Shutterstock.com: water

PHOTO CREDITS
© Bob Palosaari/Shutterstock.com: 6-7; Ethan Daniels/Shutterstock.com: 17; Giselle Luna/Shutterstock.com: cover, 1; Lee Yiu Tung/Shutterstock.com: 8-9; Maria Bobrova/Shutterstock.com: 12-13; Mauro1969/Shutterstock.com: 18; Rada Photos/Shutterstock.com: 20-21; Rich Carey/Shutterstock.com: 14-15; Seaphotoart/Shutterstock.com: 5, 11; Sek_marines/Shutterstock.com: 19

ISBN: 9781503816862
LCCN: 2016945650

Printed in the United States of America
PA02326

NOTE FOR PARENTS AND TEACHERS

The Child's World® helps early readers develop their informational-reading skills by providing easy-to-read books that fascinate them and hold their interest. Encourage new readers by following these simple ideas:

BEFORE READING

- Page briefly through the book. Discuss the photos. What does the reader think he or she will learn in this book? Let the child ask questions.
- Look at the glossary together. Discuss the words.

READ THE BOOK

- Now read the book together, or let the child read the book independently.

AFTER READING

- Urge the child to think more. Ask questions such as, "What things are different among the animals shown in this book?"

Contents

Like Plastic Bags

Something is floating in the sea. It looks like a plastic bag. But this is a sea animal. It is a jellyfish.

Did you know?

Jellyfish are often called "jellies" for short.

Not Jelly, Not Fish

Jellyfish are not fish. They are **plankton**! They ride ocean **currents**. Jellyfish move very little on their own.

Did you know?

To move, most jellyfish squeeze and push water away from their bodies.

Did you know?

Jellyfish do not have brains or hearts.

Parts of a Jellyfish

Jellyfish do not have bones. The top part of a jellyfish is called its **bell**. **Tentacles** hang from the bell.

A jellyfish's mouth is in the middle of the bell. Frilly **oral arms** push food into the mouth.

Stinging and Eating

A jellyfish's tentacles have stingers. The stingers **stun** animals. Then they are easy to catch.

Jellyfish eat shrimp and fish. They eat crabs and plants. They also eat other jellyfish.

Did you know?

Jellyfish do not hunt. They eat what floats into their tentacles.

Young Jellyfish

Adult jellyfish are called **medusas**. They **spawn** new jellyfish.

Young jellyfish grow in stages. They get new body parts at each stage. This is called **metamorphosis**.

Did you know?

There are more than 2,000 species of jellyfish.

Jellyfish Enemies

Sea turtles like to eat jellyfish. A turtle's skin is thick. A jellyfish sting does not hurt a sea turtle.

Did you know?

In China and Japan, people eat jellyfish.

Sharks and swordfish also eat jellyfish. Tuna think jellyfish are tasty, too.

Jellyfish and People

A large group of jellyfish is called a **bloom**. Some blooms can have thousands of jellyfish! A bloom can be trouble.

Did you know?

A jellyfish bloom is also called a swarm.

Jellyfish sometimes sting swimmers. The stings can hurt! Some jellyfish stings can even kill people.

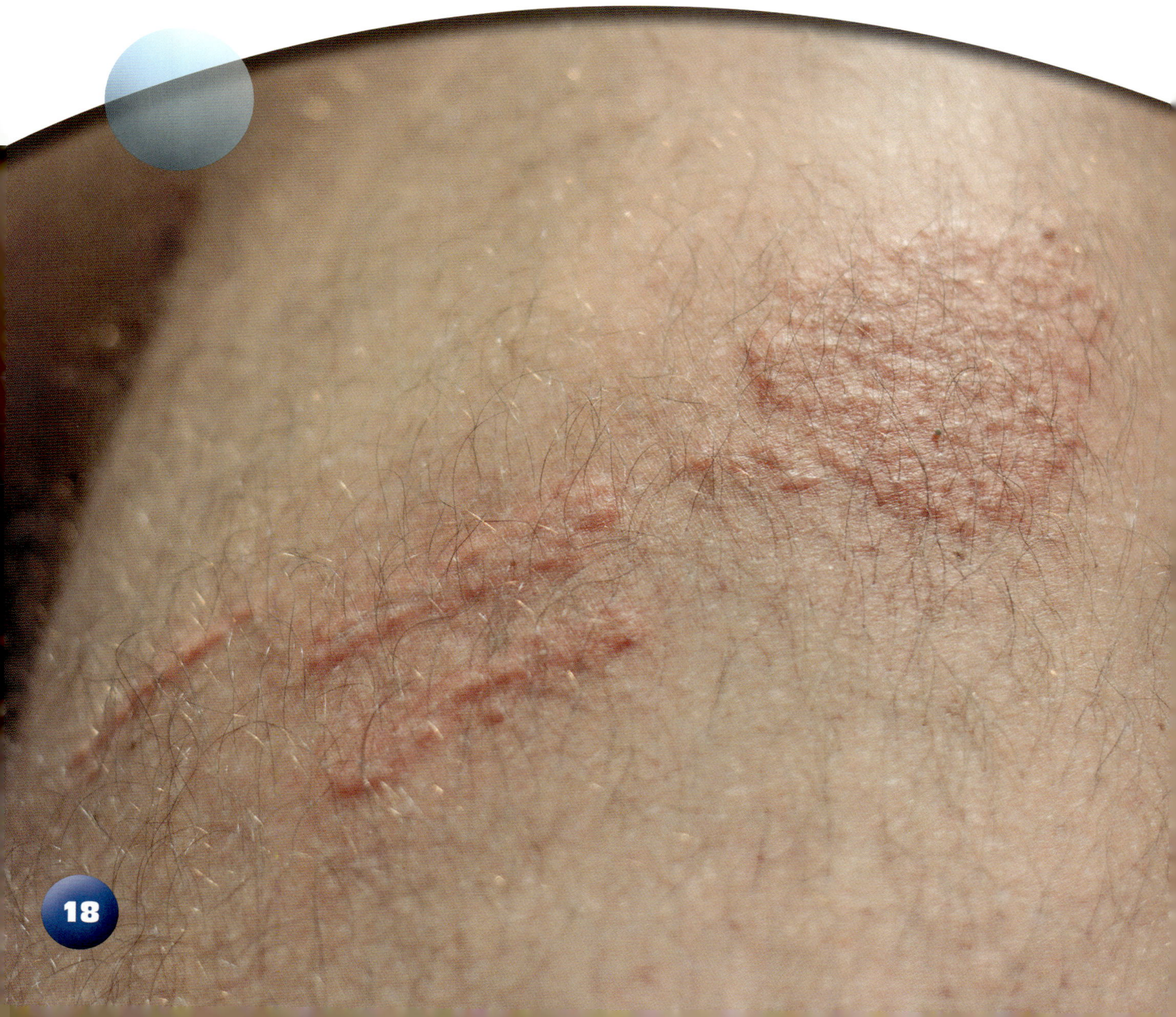

Jellyfish sometimes get stuck in fishing nets. A jellyfish bloom can be a big problem for fishermen!

Did you know?

The sea wasp jellyfish has the deadliest sting.

Jellyfish live in every part of the sea. They keep it healthy and beautiful.

Did you know?

Jellyfish live only for a few months.

GLOSSARY

bell (BEL): The top part of a jellyfish is called the bell.

bloom (BLOOM): A group of jellyfish is sometimes called a bloom.

currents (KUR-untz): Parts of the ocean where water moves in the same direction are called currents.

medusa (muh-DOO-suh): A medusa is an adult jellyfish.

metamorphosis (met-uh-MOR-fuh-sis): A series of changes some animals go through as they grow from eggs to adults is called metamorphosis.

oral arms (OR-ul ARMZ): Oral arms are the ruffled parts of a jellyfish that push food toward its mouth.

plankton (PLANK-tun): Plankton are simple ocean plants and animals. Plankton float or barely move.

spawn (SPON): When ocean animals push lots of eggs from their bodies into the sea, they spawn.

species (SPEE-sheez): A type of a certain animal. There are more than 2,000 species of jellyfish.

stun (STUN): To stun something is to make it unable to think or move for a short time.

tentacles (TENT-uh-kulz): Tentacles are long, flexible body parts that hang from some animals. Jellyfish have stinging tentacles.

TO LEARN MORE

On the Web

Visit our Web page for lots of links about jellyfish:
www.childsworld.com/links

Note to parents, teachers, and librarians: We routinely verify our Web links to make sure they are safe, active sites—so encourage your readers to check them out!

In the Library

Marsico, Katie. *Jellyfish.* New York, NY: Children's Press, 2015.

Meister, Cari. *Jellyfish.* Minneapolis, MN: Bullfrog Books, 2015.

Spilsbury, Louise. *Jellyfish.* Chicago, IL: Heinemann Library, 2011.

INDEX

About the Author

Kara L. Laughlin is an artist and writer who lives in Virginia with her husband, three kids, two guinea pigs, and a dog. She is the author of two dozen nonfiction books for kids.